D1103216

NANCY WAKE

World War Two Secret Agent
"The White Mouse"

LUCY HANNAH

Illustrations by Alex Fox

✳ SHORT BOOKS

First published in 2006 by
Short Books
15 Highbury Terrace
London N5 1UP

10 9 8 7 6 5 4 3 2 1

A CIP catalogue record for this book
is available from the British Library.

Illustration copyright © Alex Fox 2006
Quiz by Sebastian Blake

ISBN 1-904977-58-8

Printed and bound in Great Britain by
Bookmarque Ltd., Croydon, Surrey

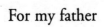

For my father

For explanations of some of the more difficult words, see the glossary at the back of the book.

THE JUMP

April 1944. A heavy wartime aeroplane made its way from England towards Nazi-occupied France. As it crossed the coast into French territory, the plane had to dodge gunfire from the German enemy guns on the ground below. Each near-miss sent the old bomber bucking through the night sky. The pilot and his navigator were used to this welcome from the enemy. But, for the two special passengers who waited in the back of the plane, this was a new experience.

One of them, a man, was thrown onto the hard metal floor as the plane rolled back and forth. The other was a glamorous woman in a camel-haired coat. She sat on the cold wooden bench. On her back was her parachute; in the pouch of her overalls was a smart leather hand-bag stuffed full of French francs for emergencies, her favourite Chanel lipstick, and two frilly nighties.

One of the plane crew, the dispatcher, sat with them. He was used to shoving parachutists out of the plane – after all, it was his job – but he hadn't seen a woman jump before. Her face was determined, and white.

'If you're scared, "Witch", we'll take you back,' the dispatcher shouted to her above the noise of the German gunfire. She'd been given the code name 'Witch,' because the plane crew weren't allowed to know who she was, or what she was going to do.

'All I want to do is get out of this bloody plane!' she yelled.

Earlier that day, a French radio operator had crouched down next to his radio receiver in a village deep in the Auvergne hills to hear a message from London. He'd relayed it to the handful of wild-looking men nearby.

'Deux anges viendrout faire de la dentelle ce soir,' he said. ('Two angels will make lace this evening.') The men, who were Maquis fighters – part of the French Resistance – had then set off for the mountains to be ready to meet the new arrivals.

The plane left the worst of the 'ack-ack' fire of the

Nazi coastal anti-aircraft guns, and headed inland. The drone of the engines made Witch feel sick. She didn't quite know what would happen if she vomited inside her oxygen mask at an altitude of 15,000 feet, but she felt sure it wouldn't be a good idea.

At last the rattle of the engines dulled slightly, and the plane slowed for the pilot to spot a signal from the French Resistance, somewhere in the valley below.

'Drop zone up ahead,' came the pilot through the intercom.

The woman pulled down her tin hat and hooked up her blue overalls. For the jump she had on her best silk stockings and regulation flat shoes. Her gold wedding ring caught the eye of the dispatcher as she adjusted the bandages around her ankles – these were to protect her bones and tendons from the impact of landing. She felt dizzy.

'You all right, love?' said the dispatcher. He didn't think it was right for a woman to be jumping out of a plane like this.

'I shouldn't have eaten those Spam rolls,' she shouted.

The dispatcher laughed. The other man checked his parachute, and prepared to jump; he was pale too.

The plane made several circles, and then pulled away

in a lazy loop before coming in to where they would make their jump. The dispatcher slid back a hatch in the floor of the plane. The wind whipped up through the hole. The three of them stared down into the gaping darkness. They could see the bonfires lit by the French Resistance to signal where they should land, and the dispatcher pointed to a discreet light flashing on and off in a field far below.

The woman was going to jump first: this had become routine during these rare missions involving female spies – it gave the men courage. The wind grabbed the legs of her overalls making an urgent flapping sound. She felt the two revolvers in her coat pockets, and took a big breath.

'Push me,' she said. The dispatcher gave her a big shove, and suddenly she was out there, falling.

She pulled frantically on the right side of her parachute, but nothing could prevent her from floating off course... she knew she was drifting away from the field with the bonfires. 'A single German bullet could rip through my open canopy at any minute,' she thought. Suddenly, she felt hard spokes around her legs, and her chute gently folded itself around her, high up, in the branches of a large tree.

She remembered her training: if you drop into a tree

keep your legs together, protect your face, and allow yourself to fall freely. She wasn't going anywhere.

'Damn,' she said. She felt the branches, and her legs. She hadn't broken anything. Then she heard a Frenchman's voice from below.

'Ah, voila un para-chute la-bas!' it said.

She drew her revolver from her coat pocket. After all he could be a German, even with a French accent.

'Ah, that England should send us such a beautiful flower,' the voice laughed.

She decided he was not about to shoot her.

'Cut out that French drivel and get me out of this tree,' she said.

The Frenchman smiled. This English woman's French was fluent; she was just what they needed. A gutsy woman whom the Germans wouldn't suspect.

'Madame Andrée?' he asked.

'Yes,' said the voice from the tree. Once on the ground she would have two code names – 'Madame Andrée' to the French Resistance, and 'Hélene' to her London headquarters. In this business, where double agents were everywhere, she couldn't ever risk using her real name – Nancy Wake.

The Frenchman deftly packed Nancy's parachute into the back of his waiting car.

'Wouldn't it be safer to bury it?' said Nancy. She carried a small shovel in her overall pocket to do just that.

'Silk like this is rare in wartime France,' he told her. 'There are many uses for it.'

'I know,' she said. 'It would make a good wedding dress – if you dyed it black.'

The Frenchman thought she was joking, but he hadn't been at Nancy's wedding. She slipped off her overalls and straightened a pretty French dress – she looked like an attractive French housewife. 'Perfect,' thought the Frenchman.

'*Bienvenue à l'Auvergne,*' he said. 'It's a bit like the Scottish Highlands.'

'But with Germans,' said Nancy.

'Yes… too many,' said the Frenchman.

'Not for long,' she said.

This woman won't let us down, he thought.

As they sped away through the moonlit mountain roads, Nancy unravelled the bandages from around her ankles, pulled out a hand-bag from the pouch in her overalls, and sat back in her seat – relieved to be back in France.

CHAPTER 1
World, here I come…

Sydney, Australia, 1918. In the back garden of a small suburban house a thin six-year-old girl in scraggy trousers and a T-shirt too big for her, perched high up in the branches of a Jacaranda tree.

'Jump!' yelled her elder brother, Stan, from the ground below.

He waited with a handful of local children, and their pet dog, as Nancy prepared herself.

'Out the way!' she shouted as she leapt from the tree into a sand-pit. Nancy's mother, Ella Wake, came out of the house to see her tomboy daughter land unscathed, but covered in sand again. The other children ran off – they were scared of Mrs. Wake, who always carried a Bible, even when she pegged out the washing. Nancy's bible was *Anne of Green Gables*, a story about an orphan who creates her own dream world.

'Just who do you think you are, Nancy Wake?' her mother said.

'I am a Hollywood stunt woman,' said Nancy.

Ella Wake often felt like giving up on the youngest and naughtiest of her six children. She was tired; she could still not quite believe that her husband, Charles, had just walked out one day and left her to bring up the children on her own. Ella was fed up with Nancy avoiding the housework to hang out at the zoo, or the beach.

'You're so like your Aunt Hinamoa,' she would shout.

'Good,' said Nancy.

Nancy longed to be like her mother's elder sister, Aunt Hinamoa, who'd run off with a whaling captain who was already married. She had never actually met this colourful relative, but she felt they would have a lot in common.

When she was young, Nancy would often escape from her mother and go to sit by the harbour with her friend.

'I am going to run away to Paris,' she said.

'You wouldn't dare!' exclaimed her friend.

'Would so,' said Nancy.

Her friend knew that nothing scared Nancy, and she was right. At sixteen Nancy did just that. She ran away from their suburban, tree-lined street and found a job as a nurse in a country town outside Sydney. She made friends with a fellow runaway, Claire, and after their shift they'd go to the pub to chat up the local miners.

'They fancy you,' said Claire.

Nancy sampled her first cigarette with aplomb. 'I think you're right.'

She'd had her hair cut short like Tallullah Bankhead – an outrageous American movie star – and scoured the magazines for the latest clothes fashions. The men looked forward to flirting with this young bundle of energy who could tell jokes as well as any of them.

While nursing in Sydney Nancy could still only fantasise about travelling abroad one day; her salary didn't give her nearly enough for such a trip. So it was a dream come true when she received a letter from Aunt Hinamoa, who'd heard that Nancy had run away, and thought she might need some financial help. In the envelope was £200 – more than enough to buy herself a first-class ticket on a cruise liner to London. Nancy was so excited she spent the rest of Aunt Hinamoa's money on two silk dresses and a beautiful pair of shoes, and danced around her room to cel-

ebrate. And so, on a gloriously sunny day in 1932, she finally waved goodbye to Sydney.

In her smart cabin on board ship, Nancy unpacked a small bag, and placed her copy of *Anne of Green Gables* on a shelf by her bunk.

The other passengers were interested in this plucky nineteen-year-old who was travelling alone.

'Aren't you scared,' an Englishwoman said, 'going all this way?'

Her husband, a professor, was more interested in European politics. 'The Nazis have become the largest political party in Germany,' he read from the newspaper. 'Nothing is going to stop that Adolf Hitler.'

'I'm following my heart,' said Nancy. 'How can you be frightened if you're doing what your heart tells you?'

Her husband looked up from his newspaper when he heard Nancy's reply. 'Spot on,' he said.

***

By the time Nancy arrived in London, her money was running out. People in London and Europe were still recovering from the effects of the First World War, and a world depression meant that jobs were scarce and everyone was feeling miserable. While Englishwomen were mainly focused on their domestic lives, Nancy enrolled on a journalism course which she hoped might find her some work. But Nancy wasn't going to let the Depression curb her appetite for fun and in the evenings she made sure she found the best value night spots.

'If we go to this place after eleven, you only need to buy one sausage and they'll let you drink as much beer as you like,' said Nancy to her new London friends.

'How do you find these places Nancy?' they'd say.

'I have a nose for it. Follow me girls!'

***

It wasn't long before Nancy secured an interview with the editor of an American newspaper who was looking for a new correspondent; Fascism was about to bring politics back into the lives of everyone in Europe.

'We need to keep our American readers informed of what's happening,' he said.

'I'll do whatever it takes,' Nancy said – she badly needed the job.

The editor had immediately warmed to this glamorous, tough-talking Australian, and he offered her the post.

'There is one problem,' he said.

Nancy's heart sank.

'You'll be based in Paris.'

Nancy put on her most serious face.

'I'm sure I can manage that.'

The editor watched his new reporter leave the building, and was mightily amused to see her throw her gloves in the air, and whoop with delight as she marched down the street.

***

In 1934, with *French for Tourists* and *Anne of Green Gables* in her suitcase, Nancy set off for Paris. She'd read that Hitler had been made supreme commander of the armed forces in Germany and, as a reporter, she knew that much of her work would involve finding out what he was planning to do.

From the moment Nancy arrived in Paris, she loved it. She made sure she wore her scarf as the French women wore theirs, she kissed people hello in the street as they did, she even bought the ultimate French accessory – a dog. In Australia, dogs were used to round up sheep. Here they were more like hand-bags. 'Picon', Nancy's wire-haired terrier (named after the French aperitif), was to be her new best friend.

Over the next few years, Nancy divided her time between her journalism, Parisian cafés, and a place that offered the most glamorous parties of all – the French Riviera in the south of France. If she was lucky, Nancy would be sent to cover a news story in the south where she would stay the night at one of the fashionable hotels in Cannes.

On one visit, she sensed that the good-looking Frenchman on the dance floor was trying to catch her eye while she danced. She'd seen him here before; he was always with a different woman.

'Who is he?' Nancy said to the barman.

'He's very rich and prefers blondes,' said the barman who liked to tease Nancy. 'Henri Fiocca, industrialist, and successful playboy.'

Nancy loved a challenge. The next time she caught Henri Fiocca glancing at her she went over to him.

'How do you do it?' she said

'Do what?' he said

'Go out with so many beautiful girls,' said Nancy.

'They ring me,' he said

'All of them?' said Nancy, surprised.

Henri laughed.

'All except the one I want to ring me.' He looked at her hard.

'I do not ring men up, they call *me*,' said Nancy.

Henri had spent far too many years dating Frenchwomen who would do anything he asked. He wanted to get to know this woman from Australia, who seemed determined to make life an adventure.

Nancy returned home to her rented studio flat in Paris, exhausted. She ran a hot bath, smoked a French cigarette, and drank a glass of French brandy. It made her throat sore, but it made her feel French. Despite the talk of war in Europe, she was happy; she felt at home here.

In the Parisian cafés she would meet Germans who had left their country because they were nervous of their new leader – Hitler. Many of these people were Jews, and, not long after her arrival in France, Nancy and her journalist friends decided to visit Vienna and Berlin, where she witnessed Nazis screaming and cracking whips at Jewish shopkeepers.

'Are you political?' asked Henri, when he came to visit Nancy in Paris.

'I wasn't until I saw that,' she said. 'Now, I am going to do whatever I can to make things difficult for that stinking Nazi Party.'

Nancy and Henri spent more and more time together in Paris, and at Henri's home in Marseilles. It all seemed unreal to Nancy: here she was in a posh apartment in the south of France with a charming, generous and good-looking lover.

'What are you thinking?' asked Henri.

'That this is mad and frivolous,' said Nancy.

'Just like you,' said Henri.

But no-one could ignore the threat of war which was becoming more real every day.

In 1939, as Hitler's forces began to advance across Europe, Henri plucked up all his courage, and asked Nancy to marry him.

CHAPTER 2
Love and War...

On a crisp November day in 1939, in one of the smart apartments in the old city of Marseilles, everyone was busy. Nancy Wake helped Marius, the chef, heave a huge frozen leg of lamb onto the kitchen table.

'Why should I eat tinned sardines on my wedding day just because of the Germans?' she asked.

Picon ran round and round the large kitchen table barking, as Nancy and Marius laughed. They'd heard on the radio how the British and the French had declared war against Germany; gas masks had been handed out; men had been called up to fight; but not much seemed to be actually happening. Marius fiddled with the radio.

'Why don't they tell us what's going on?' he said.

'The Germans invaded Poland when they said they wouldn't, and now Hitler is marching this way, and the French don't seem to realise what a monster he is,' said Nancy.

As they discussed the looming war, one of the maids arrived home with tinned food, sacks of coffee – the French couldn't manage without coffee – and lots of cigarettes, in case supplies were rationed because of the war.

The maid's mouth fell open when she saw the lamb.

'It's from Normandy, where the sheep graze on fields near salt water,' explained Marius. 'It gives them a special flavour.'

A tall, elegantly dressed Frenchman, with a big smile and a twinkle in his eye, came into the kitchen and slapped Marius on the back.

'You can afford it,' said Marius. 'He'll keep the black market afloat.'

'Oh, I will, will I?' said Henri. 'That lamb had better be good.'

Henri was what the French call a *bon viveur*; he loved his food and wine. He was also one of the most generous people in town. 'I only want the best for my little Nanny,' he said, as he gave Nancy a kiss.

On the outside, Nancy looked French with her glamorous dresses, her French cigarettes and her little canine accessory. On the inside, she was a strong and funny woman from Australia who was determined to make life an adventure. Henri was a good-looking French playboy, a rich industrialist, who'd spent many years clicking his fingers to get what he wanted. Nancy, however, would only do what she believed was right. And she was the one he wanted to marry.

'I want to hear about your wedding dress,' said Henri.

'It's black,' said Nancy. 'Silk, of course.'

'Isn't that a bit gloomy?' he said.

'It is sophisticated, isn't it Marius?' said Nancy popping an olive into Henri's mouth.

'It is beautiful, Henri,' Marius said. 'You will be very proud.'

'I will be very poor!' said Henri.

'Tell me you love me,' Henri said, as he took Nancy in his arms and looked into her big grey eyes.

Nancy kissed him, and handed him the guest list.

***

Nancy and Henri Fiocca were married in Marseilles

City Hall. Nancy wore her stunning black dress from the best clothes shop in Paris, and the wedding feast was served on grand silver plates at the local Hôtel du Louvre et Paix. Every time a new course appeared, Marius would dim the lights and the guests would stamp their feet and applaud. They had the lamb, fried sole, and beef fillets; Henri wanted the best for his new wife. All their friends from Marseilles were there, plus Nancy's friends from her days as a journalist in Paris, and Henri's father. He wasn't so happy with his eligible son marrying a loud woman with an Australian accent.

'Have you seen her dress?' he said to his friend. 'Outrageous.'

'It's silk,' his friend said.

'Black,' Henri's father said. 'And she's made him wear that ridiculous tie.'

'They are a bit of an unlikely couple,' his friend agreed.

Nancy's parents had been an unlikely couple too. Her father, Charles Wake, was a flamboyant English journalist. Ella, her mother, was a rather plain, tired-looking woman who was more likely to be found reading the Bible than doing the housework.

As they danced around the hall, Henri reassured his bride.

'Take no notice of my father,' he said.

'I gave him some wine, and sloshed a bit of vodka in it,' said Nancy. 'That should shut him up.'

'Nothing is ever dull with you, Nancy,' Henri laughed.

The Mistral wind whipped up the leaves on the pavements outside the town hall, and Notre Dame de la Gare rang out its bells in celebration. But, the war was too real, and too close, to forget altogether.

'Maybe Hitler isn't all bad?' said Henri's dad. 'I'm sure the German economy will pack up and his people will turn against him.'

'Most of France seems to have its head in the sand about this war,' said Nancy in a loud voice. 'I've seen how Hitler has bullied his people into believing his ideas – he wants to take over the world.'

'And where did you see this?' said Henri's dad, who was now a bit drunk.

'In Vienna, when I was working as a journalist, I saw Jews being publicly humiliated by Hitler's men.' She pulled up her long wedding dress and grabbed a bottle from one of the waiters. 'More wine, anyone?'

What had particularly shocked Nancy and her journalist friends was Hitler's belief that the Germans were a superior race, and they'd heard rumours of how he wanted to get rid of Jewish people. She went and sat down next to one of her friends.

'I couldn't persecute a cat, let alone a human being,' said Nancy.

'I wouldn't put it past you to thump a German, Nance,' he replied.

'Take me to him!' said Nancy.

***

The days following the wedding, were spent in a luxurious limbo for Nancy: she would have a long lie-in, bathe in expensive bath oils given to her by Henri, be brought breakfast by her maid and, after a leisurely morning, meet Henri for lunch. Marius would fill in the afternoon by teaching her to cook, 'French' style.

'I don't understand, why don't you like to cook?' Henri would ask.

'I am willing to learn,' said Nancy. 'Just don't expect me to stay in the kitchen once those Germans arrive.'

'We'll hide under the bed if they do,' said Henri.

***

As the cherry blossom was coming out on Nancy's favourite tree in May 1940, Hitler's tanks and aircraft surprised the waiting French and British troops by crossing the dense forests of the Ardennes region, and heading straight into France.

Nancy pushed open their grey bedroom shutters and stared out towards the old port. The Mistral had died down, and the narrow Marseilles streets were streaked with a clear evening light. She paced across their bedroom as the sea breeze ruffled her skirt. Henri sat on the bed, and unwrapped his soldier's uniform sent by the French army.

'I must do something,' Nancy said, pacing back and forth. 'You've been called up to fight. I must help too.'

'Calm down, Nanny,' Henri said. 'Why do you always have to be on the front line?'

'One of your factory vans would make a perfect ambulance,' said Nancy. 'Please, Henri, let me take one.'

'You're not a nurse,' Henri said.

'I am,' said Nancy. 'I was a nurse between the ages of seventeen and nineteen in Australia, after I ran away from home. I know exactly what I'm doing.'

Nancy didn't talk a lot about growing up in Australia. Her past sort of fell out, bit by bit, usually when she was convinced she had to do something.

'I can't follow my heart standing in that kitchen,' said Nancy giving Henri her determined look.

'I have no doubt about that,' he said, as he held up a greatcoat which was twice his size, and puttees from the First World War. The French did tend to look a bit scruffy in their army uniforms, compared to the polished British soldiers. Some of them actually set out to fight in their fathers' uniforms which would have been handed down from twenty years earlier.

'They expect you to fight in that?' said Nancy.

Henri dressed up in his greatcoat with Nancy's gas mask and fur-lined gloves, and they laughed so much that the neighbours came round to see what they were being so merry about. Sometimes, thought Nancy, it was easier to laugh through a really difficult moment. Deep down she was excited by the idea of her very own ambulance, it helped to her take her mind off Henri leaving.

***

Within a month, the French army was in chaotic retreat as the German tanks rolled into France. In the north of the country the British army huddled on the beaches in Dunkirk, waiting to be rescued.

Nancy joined a small voluntary ambulance unit which ferried refugees from the north of France down to safety in the south. Nancy had to avoid the German gunfire as she and the other nurses lifted the wounded men, women, and children into the back of their vans. It made Nancy angry to see these poor refugees home- less and hungry – all because of Hitler's terrible ideas. He believed that the world should be ruled by a master race of Aryan people. In Nazi politics this meant Northern European – and definitely not Jewish.

The ambulance work was tough and upsetting. However hard the nurses tried, the Germans were all around them, and Nancy's van was often bombarded by gunfire as she retreated to Marseilles with as many people as she could carry. One night, as she bumped along the roads to the south of France under a moonlit June sky, she heard the news that Paris had fallen to the Germans. The French army had collapsed, and soldiers were being sent home.

***

Back in Marseilles, Nancy slumped into her favourite chair after her exhausting drive, and fell asleep. Later that night, Picon ran to the front door when he heard the familiar footsteps of his master. Henri tip-toed across to Nancy, and gave her a big long hug.

They sat up late with a bottle of Henri's best wine, which he'd saved for emergency moments, to tell each other about their adventures.

'It was chaos,' said Henri. 'There were orders, then different orders; no-one knew what was happening.'

The Germans had taken control of most of the continental radio stations, but Nancy and Henri managed to tune in to the BBC news from London, where they heard that the whole of the north of France was now under German occupation. There were reports about how people were fleeing Paris to escape the Germans; the Government had left on the 10th of

June and Paris had fallen to the Germans on the 14th of June.

'Those Germans are animals,' Nancy said. 'I can't imagine how human beings can behave like that.'

A line was to be drawn between the north and the south of France. A French First World War hero, called Henri Philippe Pétain, was put in charge of a new Government in Vichy, a spa town in the southern part – which was now referred to as 'Vichy France'. The Germans occupied the north.

'All our politicians are squabbling, it's embarrassing,' said Henri.

'I don't trust Pétain,' said Nancy. 'He's pretty much agreed to work with the Germans.'

As they huddled close together on the sofa that hot summer evening, they heard Charles de Gaulle, the leader of the 'Free French', come on the radio. He'd fled to England to continue the fight against Hitler.

'The flame of the French Resistance must never go out,' de Gaulle's voice crackled through the radio.

'Hear, hear,' said Nancy. 'At least he's not going to give up.'

'He'll hate it in London,' said Henri. 'They've rationed butter; de Gaulle loves butter, poor fellow.'

Nancy and Henri always found something to laugh

about. The news was interrupted by a high-pitched whirring noise. This was to become a regular sound; the Germans didn't want people knowing what was really going on.

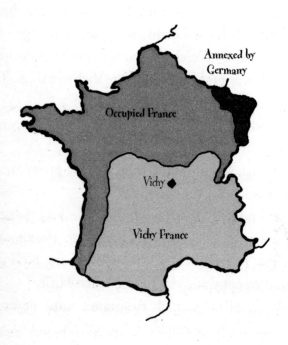

CHAPTER 3

'Freedom is the only thing worth living for. While I was doing
that work I used to think it didn't matter if I died, because
without freedom there was no point in living.'
Nancy Wake, Sydney Morning Herald

Marseilles, with its many colourful streets and
its busy fish and flower markets, suddenly
became a place of curfews, distrust and
queues for food rations. Even though it wasn't occupied, the south of France seemed to have German
informers in every district. Nancy and Henri didn't
know whether to trust their neighbours, or even some
of their friends.

'It's a scandal,' said Nancy.

'Keep your voice down,' said Henri.

'I don't care if they hear me.'

Nancy didn't feel she could just stand by and watch Hitler's army destroy the country. Many, many Jews had fled from Hitler in Germany, but his army had caught up with them in France and there'd been mass arrests of Jews in Paris. It was unjust and, if anything made Nancy really angry, it was injustice.

By July 1940, Hitler's army had taken control of Europe. Britain and Germany made bombing air-raids on each other; planes flew across the Channel every night to destroy strategic buildings in the great cities. Meanwhile in London, the British Prime Minister, Winston Churchill, set up the Special Operations Executive, or the SOE, to send secret agents into occupied territory (much of mainland Europe) to gather secret intelligence about the Germans. Secret groups also began to form across France to gather information to use against the German occupiers, and the Vichy Government – which was collaborating with the Germans and therefore didn't represent real freedom for the French.

Often, in the early evening, Nancy would go to the Hôtel du Louvre et Paix, and wait for Henri to join her. He'd make her wait for him in the back bar in case she decided to sing *Rule Britannia* in a loud voice, which she had done once – it had not gone down well with the Vichy police, and even less well with the visiting German officers. One evening she started chatting to a French soldier.

'Pétain's Vichy Government is not going to protect us from the Germans, you know,' he said.

'He's made a truce.' Nancy was careful what she said; she didn't know where this conversation was leading.

'He is a puppet,' the soldier said.

'Can you keep a secret?' he said, quietly, as they sipped their drinks.

He was a member of one of these secret 'Resistance' groups. Nancy, he said, had the perfect 'cover' – or disguise – to help his group; as Madame Fiocca, the glamorous wife of a Marseilles businessman, she was unlikely to be stopped and searched by the Vichy police. The Resistance leaders knew that she would have a better chance than any man of smuggling a radio set, or carrying key information along the coast for them.

'Ever since I told on a girl at school, I have vowed never to betray anyone ever again,' said Nancy.

The French soldier was impressed.

'This is not schoolgirl pranks,' he said.

'I'll do anything to get rid of the Germans,' said Nancy. 'I believe what they are doing is wrong.'

'But if you are caught, they may shoot you,' said the soldier.

He explained that he worked across the south of France for Commander Busch, code-named Xavier, whose Resistance group printed anti-German leaflets, and helped captured Allied servicemen to escape from France

'Tell me what to do,' said Nancy, ordering them both another gin and tonic.

The French officer asked her to take an envelope for him to Cannes. At first Nancy had no idea what she was carrying, but the more often she made these errands, the more the Resistance group trusted her. A friendly doctor made her a French identity card – her English ID papers would have made the Germans question her, which would also have put Henri at risk, and she didn't want to do anything that would put him in danger.

But Henri was against the idea. 'It's not right for my wife to be doing this kind of work,' he said.

'You'd better get to know your wife,' said Nancy.

Henri couldn't take part in active Resistance work because it was important for him to keep running his business.

'It's dangerous,' he said.

'It's important,' said Nancy

'I know,' said Henri. 'I just worry.'

Soon, Nancy was ferrying radio transmitters and maps to couriers in other towns, so that the Resistance could send information to London which would help them surprise the German army.

While French women spent most of their day queuing up for food, Nancy would cycle miles to deliver packages – the bicycle was the most common form of transport for couriers like her. For longer trips she would take the train, and sit reading a French magazine in her most expensive clothes. If the Vichy police searched the train, she would flutter her eyelashes and flirt with them; she would then dodge the electricity cuts, and the curfews, to find her way home to their apartment.

'I should have been an actress,' she told Henri; 'In Marseilles I am Madame Fiocca, your wife and a society hostess. Up and down the coast I have to pretend to be Mademoiselle Lucienne Carlier, secretary to a doctor, to cover up my true identity.'

'This is not some *Anne of Green Gables* adventure,' Henri said. 'Hitler is on the hunt for all foreign-born and French-born Jews.'

'All the more reason for me to do this work,' said Nancy. 'I distracted a policeman by offering him a date the other day.'

'Be careful, Nancy. Please,' implored Henri.

'Don't worry,' said Nancy. 'I know how to keep them guessing.'

'That's what worries me,' said Henri. 'What are we going to do with this brave mad woman, Picon?'

Picon just barked at him.

***

One starless evening, a rather good-looking Scotsman came to eat at Nancy and Henri's apartment. Despite the strict food rations, they kept up their entertaining; Nancy was a bit of a demon on the black market and the shopkeepers would try their best to find what she needed.

'It's important to keep up morale,' she said to the Scotsman.

'I agree,' he said. 'You can't fight a war on an empty stomach.'

Captain Ian Garrow was from the big fort in Marseilles. It was here that the Vichy Government held captured Allied soldiers (on the British side) – they were allowed to wander around the town, but they were not allowed to leave.

By 1941 the war had spread further throughout the world and some of the British army was needed to fight the Italians in North Africa. Captain Garrow's project was to help his soldiers to escape from Marseilles by going over the Pyrenees Mountains into Spain, and then on to England. They would then be able to rejoin their fellow soldiers wherever they were needed.

'There's no point having Allied soldiers sitting about in a fort, just waiting,' he quietly explained to Nancy. 'I've organised an escape route. It's a line of safe houses all the way from here to the foot of the Pyrenees.'

Nancy liked Garrow; she would stay up late into the night listening his stories of war and escape. After he left, Nancy sat down with Henri.

'He needs radio transmitters, cigarettes, food, and ration cards for the soldiers' escape. And trusty friends on the outside of the fort,' said Nancy.

'Like you,' said Henri.

'Like us,' said Nancy.

'He drinks too much,' said Henri.

'All Scots drink whiskey,' said Nancy.

'What makes you such an authority on the Scots?' asked Henri, surprised.

'I have travelled, and I know,' she kissed him. 'Will you help Garrow?'

'It sounds ludicrously romantic,' said Henri.

'Well, you are a romantic,' said Nancy. 'And he needs our help.'

Henri donated one of his factories for the escapees to spend their first night in. While continuing her courier work for the French Resistance, Nancy also now began to escort soldiers towards the Pyrenees for Captain Garrow.

She fast became a key link in the escape line, but wasn't told who else was in the line of guides. It was the safest way to operate; the more you knew, the harder it would be if you were questioned by the military police. And as the war escalated in the north of the country, the police were becoming much more suspicious of everybody.

Listening to the BBC on the radio was the only way to find out what was really going on in the war. The streets of Marseilles would empty when it was time for the news. Try as hard as they could, the Germans couldn't blot it out completely. People heard that the

Germans' bombing air-raids on London were causing a huge amount of damage. The British press called these frequent, and heavy, raids the 'Blitz' – which was the German word for 'lightning'. They were trying to destroy morale in Britain before a planned invasion.

***

To her friends and neighbours, Nancy was still Madame Fiocca, housewife – despite her secret work

'It's crucial that the escapees don't know your name and who you really are,' said Garrow one evening.

Although Nancy was very discreet, some of Garrow's men hadn't taken to this outspoken Australian.

'Try not to be so exuberant,' said Garrow quietly. 'Some of the men are worried that you're a security risk.'

'Well "Some of the men", will have to put up with it,' said Nancy. 'We're all at risk.'

'You especially – we've heard the Germans are looking for a woman fitting your description,' said Garrow.

Although Vichy France was not occupied, the Nazis had bands of secret police, known as the Gestapo, controlling France. What Garrow told Nancy was that the Paris branch of the Gestapo had been tipped off about a dark-haired woman smuggling key information. She was codenamed 'The White Mouse' – because she was so hard to catch.

If the Marseilles Gestapo and the Paris Gestapo had compared notes at the time, they might have realised that this 'White Mouse' was actually the dizzy wife of a French industrialist, and that her real name was Madame Fiocca. But, luckily for Nancy, they were too competitive to think of joining forces. Garrow and Nancy knew that all the evidence pointed to her. She had to be especially careful.

'I just don't want to see you caught,' said Garrow.

'Or the escape line jeopardised,' said Nancy.

'Quite,' said Garrow.

It was hard work for Nancy: she often had to wait alone for many hours until the servicemen escaping from Marseilles were handed over to her by another guide. On a cheerier note she made regular visits along the coast to a safe house in Nice run by a Madame Sainson, whom she liked very much. On one of these visits, Nancy teased Madame about the huge artificial flowers in the kitchen: 'Marseilles has one of the best flower markets in Europe,' said Nancy. 'I could bring you a fresh bunch.'

'You could give buttonholes to the vicious Vichy,'

said a laughing Madame Sainson.

'Do you think it's possible to laugh your way through the Occupation?' Nancy asked.

Suddenly, they heard police shouting outside, and knocking on the doors of neighbours' flats. The Germans were looking for those they believed were hostile to their regime.

'Police Allemande!'

Nancy clambered into one of Madame Sainson's wardrobes to hide.

'It's the only way to survive,' said Madame Sainson, as she shut the door.

***

Living under Vichy Government made everyone, particularly the Jews, fear a knock at the door from the Germans. Occasionally, Nancy was asked to help a family to escape. She tried not to be drawn into their stories, but sometimes it was tricky. Beneath the tough exterior, Nancy was soft as they come. She liked to carry black market biscuits for the children.

'Do you have a baby?' a child would ask.

'No, but I have a lovely husband,' she would reply.

'Do you have brothers and sisters?'

'Yes,' Nancy would whisper, as they hid in a warehouse waiting for a signal to make their next move.

'Where are they?'

'Australia.'

'Where's that?'

'A long, long way away,' Nancy would say.

When Nancy returned home to Marseilles after one of her missions, Picon, who always slept in the same big leather arm chair, was as relieved as Henri to see her. They cracked open a tin of powdered milk, and had a cup of *café nationale*, horrid-tasting rationed coffee. Britain had blockaded food supplies to France in case the Germans stole it, and the Vichy government had banned alcohol for part of the week which made Henri really angry.

'I hate this powdered milk,' said Henri. He loved fresh milk and he loved butter, but that was scarce now, too. They'd decided to save any real coffee, or tobacco, so that in an emergency they could sell it on the black market.

Nancy and Henri's peace was suddenly broken by the sound of German troops arriving outside their neighbours' home.

'*Ah! Mais c'est pas possible!* This is our home, leave us alone!' the neighbours yelled at the soldiers.

The Germans took no notice and set fire to the flat. Nancy had to stop Picon barking, because he smelt the smoke; he hated the smell of smoke.

'I want to help them,' she said.

'You are not going anywhere,' said Henri placing his hand on her shoulder. 'You're a wanted woman.'

'Police Allemande!' the Germans shouted.

They heard their neighbours being bundled into a truck, to be taken to the police station; their home was destroyed.

'Those absolute pigs,' said Nancy, as they huddled together.

'They pull out their prisoners' teeth, and beat them senseless,' said Henri. 'I can't bear to think of you being tortured by them.'

'If they caught me, they might stick pins in my breasts,' said Nancy. 'They do that to women spies, apparently. But a Maori midwife in New Zealand told my mother I would always be lucky.'

'Let's hope she's right,' said Henri.

'She has been so far,' said Nancy.

***

Part of Nancy's work was to ask for loans from French businessmen to fund the escape line. She would prove that she was working for the British Government, and that it would pay them back, by using codes. Nancy would ask the lender to think of a silly phrase like, 'The crow flies backwards in Norfolk,' and tell them to listen to the BBC News the next night. She would then make sure that the same phrase was broadcast in the 'personal messages' section, which came after the news. This was how they knew she was to be trusted. When she couldn't raise the money, Nancy would ask Henri for help.

'Another one for the Scots, eh Nanny?' Henri would ask, as he bankrolled another escape operation.

'It's for a good cause,' said Nancy. 'And we've run out of fuel, again.' There was never enough fuel for heating during the war.

'We shall just have to keep each other warm then,' said Henri.

***

Nancy had been working for the 'Garrow line' for almost a year when she heard that Captain Garrow had been betrayed, and captured by the Gestapo. No-one believed that Garrow would crack under torture, but he would be beaten and possibly even given a lethal injection.

Garrow's capture made Nancy all the more determined to keep working with Captain Pat O'Leary, co-leader of the escape line. The network had grown from barely 30 people to more than a hundred now. Nancy found O'Leary a bit too bossy, but, before working with Nancy, he had masterminded the tunnelling escape of 37 Allied airmen from a military prison near Nice, which made her respect him. She now split her time between routine escape-line work with O'Leary, and thinking of clever ways to get Garrow out of jail. Pretending to be his upset and glamorous first cousin, Nancy visited him as much as she could. They would talk quietly, so the dozy security guard couldn't hear.

'What's happening?' said Garrow.

'The Blitz; the Japanese attacked Pearl Harbor; the Americans have joined the war,' whispered Nancy. 'That's all we hear, but they keep jamming the radio.'

'Not a good time to be a wanted woman,' said Garrow, concerned.

Garrow appreciated Nancy's visits. After three months, he was moved to Meauzac concentration camp. Nancy and Henri went to Marseilles station to try to catch sight of him. They saw their emaciated friend dragging his prison chains behind him.

'We'll just have to break into the camp and get him out,' Nancy said.

'It's a prison, not a shop,' said Henri.

'I have a hunch they might be open to a small financial bribe,' said Nancy.

'You can't…'

'Watch me,' Nancy said. 'I know those guards can be bought.'

Nancy's elaborate escape plan for Garrow involved visiting him every week to flaunt her money at the guards. Henri continued to fund his wife's crazy bribery scheme, and the guards fell for it. Garrow sneaked out wearing a guard's uniform smuggled in by Nancy and escaped back to England along his own escape line.

***

The following year, in November 1942, the Germans marched across the demarcation line between the north of France and the Vichy south. In Marseilles there were now the Gestapo and the French gendarmes, who were sent to hunt down foreign refugees with batons and hoses, as well as the black market police and the German occupying troops. The Vichy government in the south of France had always been on the Germans' side, and now they set up yet another police unit called the Milice, specially to combat the Resistance. This just made the Resistance fighters more frantic to continue their work.

Following one of her courier trips, Nancy was told by a friend that she was being followed. If the Gestapo were really this close to her, they would be watching to see where she went, and to see who else she spoke to. She knew that, from now on, the Milice or the Gestapo could be waiting for her in any one of the many twists and turns of the streets of Marseilles, but she insisted on carrying on her work.

She would pop into the apartment to see Henri when she could, but it wasn't safe to stay there overnight any more; the Germans made midnight arrests when people were half asleep. Nancy dodged from safe house to safe house.

Nancy didn't mind staying in unexpected places; nothing would ever be as bad as having had to share her mother's bed after her father left home. Then, she had lain awake and plotted her escape from Australia. Now, she lay awake and plotted her escape from Marseilles, except this time, she didn't want to leave.

The Gestapo were making public arrests of Jews on the streets of Marseilles – they were getting close to Nancy.

One crisp December afternoon, Nancy realised she was running out of places to take cover; being in Marseilles was too dangerous for her, and for Henri. A neighbour was now known to have contacts in the police, and he'd been watching Nancy's movements.

'You have to go, Nanny.' Henri couldn't look at her when he said this. He didn't want to lose her. 'Every minute counts.'

'I know,' she said. 'I know.'

They agreed that he should stay to look after his business and join her in England as soon as he could; it was safer that way. She packed her jewellery in her handbag. They hid behind the doorway to say goodbye. Picon barked.

'He knows I'm not coming back,' Nancy said, trying her hardest to be brave and not to cry. 'This is dreadful, Henri.'

'I'll be with you very soon,' said Henri.

He stared at Nancy and wondered how he'd come to

choose such a driven woman. He kissed her.

'*Au revoir, chérie,*' he said.

'Hopefully not *adieu*,' said Nancy.

'Always *au revoir*,' Henri whispered, as they walked towards the front door.

Opposite the apartment, a military policeman paced up and down the pavement.

'Back soon,' Nancy said.

She flounced onto the street as if she was taking a stroll, and cried all the way to the station; she had wanted to say so much to Henri, but there hadn't been time. O'Leary escorted Nancy along the escape line, via the safe houses she knew so well, to the foothills of the Pyrenees.

Over the previous two and a half years Nancy had helped just over a thousand evaders escape to safety in England. Her own escape wasn't going to be so easy.

CHAPTER 4

"She had no fear." A school friend of Nancy

Nancy sat in a cold, dark, prison cell in Toulouse. She could hear the guards laughing outside her door, and smell the smoke of their cigarettes which made her feel sick. The Germans hadn't given her anything to eat or drink for four days; she felt weak, and didn't know how she would cope once they started to interrogate her.

'Damn,' thought Nancy. 'Damn, damn, damn.'

As she lay in her cell counting the marks on the ceiling, she hoped that the Toulouse Gestapo didn't work out that she was the elusive 'White Mouse'. If they found exactly who she was they might send her to a prison camp where they burned 'spies' like her in ovens, or left them in refrigerators for hours to make them talk.

After she left Henri in Marseilles, Nancy had made three attempts to cross the Pyrenees, and eventually escape to England, but had failed each time because of high winds and blizzards; she'd gone back to Toulouse to wait for better weather. But, while avoiding the Milice by going down a side street, she had become caught up with some demonstrators, and arrested by another set of police. Her captors accused her of being a local prostitute; they had been hunting for a 'good-looking woman' on the streets, and, given their laziness, it was easier to arrest Nancy. She'd managed to eat an English pound note she'd had in her bag – a memento from one of her escapees – before they searched her, but she knew the proper interrogation was yet to come.

When, after four long days, she was dragged from her cell into the bright sunlight, she saw a line of German guards, and O'Leary. He walked towards her and kissed her hard.

'They think you're my mistress,' he whispered. 'For God's sake, kiss me.'

She'd never warmed to O'Leary as much as Garrow, but she was so relieved to see him that even the Germans seemed a little embarrassed by their long embrace.

O'Leary had pleaded with them to let his mistress free, and they'd fallen for it.

'What took you so long?' said Nancy as they left the police station.

'I waited to see if they came to disrupt the escape line; when they didn't, I knew you hadn't talked and there was a chance of getting you out,' he said.

'I would never talk,' said Nancy.

'Wait until they pull out all your toenails,' he said. Secretly, O'Leary was impressed by Nancy. But he never let it show.

She was desperate to leave France now; if she was in France she wanted to be with Henri, not holed up in a safe house, never managing to escape. But she had to wait for a handful of prisoners to join her, before making another attempt to scale the mountains. An untidy collection of soldiers sent by O'Leary soon arrived.

'Clothes off,' Nancy would say to each of them.

'No, please,' said a rather tired-looking French soldier.

'Yes, please,' said Nancy. If they weren't going to

clean themselves up, she'd have to do it for them. Dirty clothes were a sure way to be stopped and searched. All kitted out they split into two groups to make their way across Toulouse, trying to look innocent as they passed groups of Gestapo. Nancy clutched her handbag close.

'What's in the bag?' O'Leary asked.

'Essentials,' said Nancy.

An engagement ring, a three-carat solitaire diamond, a diamond eternity ring, a diamond watch, a diamond brooch in the shape of a little wire-haired terrier, and some gold bracelets probably weren't seen to be essential to O'Leary, but they were to Nancy. She wasn't leaving the country without her presents from Henri. On the train out of Toulouse, O'Leary sighed, and sat back in his seat.

'You should make it this time,' he said.

'I'll crawl over those mountains, if I have to,' said Nancy.

Almost as she said this, the train slowed down and a troop of military police boarded. In panic Nancy grabbed her handbag; O'Leary leapt up and yanked down the train window.

'Jump,' he shouted to the group.

Nancy pushed herself out of the window, and leapt.

She thudded onto the rough ground by the tracks; she heard a screech as the train lurched to a halt above her, then rolled fast down the stony bank, spitting out grit as she went. Over and over – she tried to keep curled up, and stopped suddenly against a vine. She felt her legs; they were still working, but as soon as she moved, she heard bullets whizz past her head; they pinged onto the vine wood as she ran, head down, through the vineyard to a nearby wood.

Something was missing. Her bag!

'Bloody Germans,' said Nancy to herself. She couldn't bear the thought of them finding her jewellery.

She checked inside her bra, where she'd hidden some money, at least that was still there. And her wedding ring was still on.

O'Leary led them across country; they slept in barns and soon smelled of sweat and dirt. The 'White Mouse' was cold, and hungry; she wanted to lie next to Henri and for it all to be over.

Eventually they reached a safe house in the foothills. It was the soldiers' turn to get their own back on Nancy now; she had developed scabies, a skin disease, which meant they had an excuse to strip off her clothes and scrub her down with disinfectant.

'Clothes off,' they said.

Nancy shrieked as they slopped cold mountain water over her.

'Close your eyes while you do it,' shouted Nancy. 'Ouch!'

O'Leary went to the nearby village to meet their mountain guide, but his contact had betrayed him and the Gestapo were lying in wait in the village. All the escapees knew that O'Leary had huge courage, and that he would never talk, even if it meant death, but they would now have to travel via Marseilles to warn the rest of O'Leary's network about his arrest. Nancy pulled herself up, and led the party to the train station. The station at Marseilles, so familiar to Nancy, made her stomach feel funny. After they had alerted their people, they moved on to Nice to take refuge with Madame Sainson while they waited for new forged ID cards.

O'Leary had been the only one who knew where to find their guide for the Pyrenees; but Nancy remembered O'Leary going to a particular house, and she was so fed up now that she decided to risk it, and led the others back to the mountains. Without the right code word, the plan could go horribly wrong.

A rugged-looking man opened the door of the house.

'I work for O'Leary and so do you. I want to go to

Spain, and you're in charge of our guides. I've had enough trouble getting out here so don't give me any crap,' Nancy said.

It worked. They climbed into the back of coal lorries, and hid under coal sacks, to go through the German check points to the bottom of the snowy mountain path. They wore espadrilles, French canvas shoes, which didn't make a sound crossing the rocks, and made sure they climbed across the highest, hardest boulders – they could hear the Germans below them, but they knew that their sniffer dogs couldn't go across these stones. Every couple of hours they had to remove their wet socks to avoid getting frostbite.

In the middle of a blizzard one of their party sat down and refused to go on.

'Keep moving!' Nancy shouted.

'I can't,' he said.

'Do you want to die?' Nancy said. 'Do want us to leave you?'

The man shook his head but still didn't move. Nancy grabbed hold of his hair and dragged him along the path. She didn't care what he thought of her; he wasn't going to ruin their chances of escape.

Nancy realised that, during the last few months, she had left some of her dizzy, flirty self behind in Marseilles; she had become a rather different, fiercer woman.

***

As the spring flowers were opening on the foothills of the Pyrenees, almost six months after she had left Henri, Nancy walked down a grassy slope and into a safe house on the Spanish side of the mountains. She removed her sodden socks, and lay down in the sunlight. Before long, they would be in Madrid, where Nancy could buy silk blouses, and silk stockings, to wear on the boat ride home.

And so, at last, back to England. 'Passport, please,' a bored official said to Nancy at the British port.

'Passport!?' she said.

'You haven't the correct papers for entry, madam,' he said.

'You're lucky we're here at all,' said Nancy.

She managed to send a message to Captain Garrow, in London, to help sort out the confusion. When Nancy eventually got there he took her out to dinner at a smart London restaurant, to calm her down. Nancy was so happy to see him, she sang *Waltzing Matilda* in a loud voice.

'This wine tastes like gnat's piss,' Nancy said.

'Do we have to have an "Australian moment", here?' said Garrow, who was used to these outbursts. He enjoyed Nancy's company, and he was eager to talk about the escape network in Marseilles.

'O'Leary has been sent to Dachau concentration camp,' Garrow said.

Nancy was silent. Dachau was one of the harshest German concentration camps.

'It has wooden beating racks,' said Nancy.

'He's the most courageous soldier I know,' said Garrow. 'We can only hope and wait. The Germans have suffered a set-back with Stalingrad in Russia, and we think the Italians and Germans will surrender in North Africa soon.' Garrow was always up to date on the war situation.

***

London in 1943 wasn't the party place Nancy remembered from the early 1930s, when she had been fresh off the boat from Sydney. Londoners were in their fourth year of war: buildings she knew had been flattened by German bombs, and the park railings had been melted down to make ammunition. There were constant black-outs, air-raid warnings and the rationing was extreme.

Nancy decided to rent a flat and wait for Henri to join her. She found one in the centre of town, and tried to make it feel like home. But nowhere was home without Henri, and Picon; she missed them so much. She bought a bottle of French champagne and French brandy, to keep for when he arrived.

The reunions were over between herself and her refugees from the Garrow and O'Leary network – they all had their own lives now – and Nancy felt a sort of 'what am I going to do next' loneliness. She would cheer herself up by singing along to *Kiss the Boys Goodbye* with Anne Shelton on the radio. Nancy would put on her best French frock, smear gravy browning on her legs in place of stockings – which were hard to find during the war – and go to see *Gone with the Wind* at the cinema. English women were urged to dress well, and wear make up (even though cosmetics were rationed) to keep morale high.

A friend soon found her some voluntary work in a canteen, but being surrounded by upper-class English ladies doing their bit for the war effort didn't suit Nancy.

'You sound as if you're from Australia,' one of them said.

'New Zealand,' Nancy said. 'Then Australia. I left there when I was nineteen, and went to live in Paris.'

'Quite the nomad,' one of the others remarked, as she poked Nancy's limp Victoria sponge with a knife. 'A nomad who can't cook.'

'Is that all you care about?' said Nancy, trying not to lose her temper with these smug women.

'We're all doing our bit, darling,' the woman said. 'This is more fun for us girls than being stuck at home all day.'

'Do you know what those Nazis are doing?' said Nancy, trying to control her rage.

The previous night Nancy had had a nightmare about Henri being tortured by the Germans; she couldn't stand these posh English women one moment longer.

'Oh, keep your pinnies!' said Nancy.

She stormed out of the canteen to find work which she felt would make a *real* difference in the fight against the Nazis.

CHAPTER 5

"Set Europe Ablaze," Churchill's instructions to the SOE
(Special Operations Executive)

The small bare room with its naked light bulb didn't frighten Nancy. A thin, pale Englishman called Jepsom paced around her in circles as he talked.

'We've heard all about you and your work on the escape lines,' he said. 'You're just the type we're looking for.'

'And what would that be?' said Nancy.

'Your French is fluent, you understand the French way of life, you're fearless, and will do anything to help France. Am I right?'

'I think those Nazis need a bloody good kicking,' said Nancy.

'Precisely,' said Jepsom. 'I couldn't have put it better myself.'

He was a thriller writer who was employed by the Special Operations Executive to spot the people who would make the best secret agents.

The SOE was set up to work with the Resistance to provide intelligence about the Germans, but now its main job was to sabotage the Nazi soldiers and carry out guerrilla warfare against them from inside France and the rest of occupied Europe – this was armed resistance. Its selection process was as mysterious as much of its work. Its female agents included a professional dancer, a fashion designer, and a princess. Captain Garrow had suggested they contact Nancy, before she upset any more Englishwomen. This type of work was much more her style.

'Why do you love France so much?' Jepsom asked her.

'My husband is French, my dog is French, I feel French,' she said.

'Were you afraid, in France?' Jepsom asked.

'I was too busy to be afraid,' said Nancy.

Even the sceptical Jepsom couldn't fail to be intrigued by this gutsy, sensuous woman who had such a will to fight.

'Do you feel loyal to this country?' said Jepsom.

'In Sydney, aged seven, I'd be dressed up in my best hand-me-down clothes for Anzac Day to remember the Australian and New Zealand soldiers who died during the First World War. My brother, Stan, fought in that one.'

'That doesn't mean anything.' Jepsom stared into Nancy's eyes.

'Look mate,' she said. 'I was brought up in a family where, although we were from New Zealand and living in Australia, we were "of" Great Britain, and we were loyal to whoever was on the throne. It was never something you questioned.'

'What we do here at the SOE, Nancy, is dangerous work,' said Jepsom. 'We would drop you by parachute into occupied France. If you work for us, you have about a fifty-fifty chance of coming out of the war alive. Many of our agents are captured by the Germans, treated as spies, and shot.'

'I'm lucky,' said Nancy.

Jepsom turned away from her to the window, which overlooked a bomb-damaged London street.

'I have no doubt,' he said, 'that "The White Mouse" will always be lucky.'

As Nancy left the building an air-raid siren sounded.

She knew without any further thought that this was the job for her.

For her secret service training, Nancy was given a smart British army uniform – she was now officially part of the British Army's First Aid Nursing Yeomanry – her style was more silk and chiffon than beret and tie, but she looked handsome in her soldier's kit. She joined a group of SOE trainees which included Poles, French, and French Canadians, plus an American agent who'd been a Hollywood stunt man.

It was tough work. They were sent on courses to learn how to break into buildings, how to get out of handcuffs, how to resist interrogation, how to use codes and passwords, and how to parachute. Nancy was given lessons in how to use a revolver, and a Bren gun, and how to handle grenades.

Nancy sat staring at what looked like a rat.

'It is a rat... well, rat's skin,' said an SOE boffin. 'With an explosive inside.'

'An exploding rat!' said Nancy.

'For blowing up ammunition bases,' said the boffin. 'Good disguise, eh?'

The SOE scientists showed them corks with hidden compartments, pretend tree trunks where they could hide their own ammunition and,

Nancy's favourite, a cigarette pistol.

'It has just one shot,' said the scientist.

'I won't miss my target,' said Nancy.

They were given sleeve guns and the men had tubes of shaving cream with a hidden compartment. They learned how to 'Frenchify' themselves: to comb their hair, and use a knife and fork, like the French. They even had their teeth fillings replaced with French-looking ones.

There was one problem with the course in Scotland where they learned how to parachute.

'Where's the gin?' said Nancy.

'Only beer here,' said the barman.

'I'm from France,' said Nancy. 'I drink spirits, or wine.'

'Beer or nothing love,' he said.

'I shall just have to struggle through a few pints of bitter then,' said Nancy.

And struggle she did. She soon found she could match the men's drinking pint for pint. Her group went down in the record book for the most alcohol consumed on the course.

One day, when she was being taught how to make explosives, Nancy met Violette Szabo. She was a young and beautiful War widow, who was to become a famous resistance fighter. Nancy couldn't resist a few practical jokes. One day, to liven up a session, she and Violette stole a pair of trousers from an instructor and hoisted them up a flagpole.

'You are wicked Nancy,' said Violette as they waited for the instructor to see them.

'Wake!' he shouted. 'Is this some kind of Australian joke?'

'Just practising my ambush skills,' said Nancy.

A couple of the men fell in love with the beautiful Violette, and the four of them – the two men, Violette and Nancy – would go out drinking and dancing when they had a night off. That was when Nancy missed Henri the most, when other couples were dancing together on the dance floor. She loved dancing with Henri. She had to remind herself that she was doing something that really mattered, and she was having fun with her new friends. But they all knew that they'd soon be split into groups of three – each group would include a radio operator (their lifeline back to London), an agent and a courier, for their various missions across occupied France.

'I wonder if we'll survive,' said Violette.

'The men are more at risk than us,' said Nancy. 'With over a million and a half Frenchmen in prisoner-of-war camps, any fit young man'll look out of place.'

'Volunteering is easy,' said Violette, staring deep into her glass. 'It's what goes on in your heart before you volunteer.'

'To our hearts,' said Nancy raising her glass.

***

Not long after she began the Secret Service training, Nancy wrote a letter to Henri, and gave it to Garrow. Henri would be sure to try to contact her via the old network, if he made it to London; he had no address or number for her. She wasn't allowed to write about what she was doing in France, but she was able to tell him about the flat, and how he shouldn't worry about her, and that she'd join him again very soon.

Nancy was teamed with Denis Rake, known as 'DenDen', a colourful wireless operator, and Major John Farmer, an upright British army officer who had to admit that he found Nancy rather vulgar on occasions; just his luck that he was to be dropped behind enemy lines with the mad Australian. But he knew that women spies were very useful to the SOE, especially in France, where women were not such obvious suspects.

DenDen wasn't going to parachute in with them.

'Chicken,' said Nancy.

'Darling,' said DenDen. 'Call me what you like, but I am not going to jump out of one of those things ever again.'

As one of the SOE's most valuable, and experienced, radio operators he could say how he wanted to travel; he would go in a small landing aircraft and join Nancy and Major Farmer there.

Nancy was given false French identity documents, and a 'cover' story to pretend that she was a genuine French citizen,

'Your name is the most important thing to remember,' said the instructor. 'Never mind forgetting your age, or your accent – those you might get away with, but you must be consistent with your name.'

Nancy didn't have a great memory, so she picked an Australian limerick to identify herself to London headquarters; this was her key SOE code. Most people chose something from the Bible or Shakespeare, but the limerick was the only thing she could be sure of remembering:

She stood right there
In the Moonlight fair,

And the moon shone,
Through her nightie,
It lit right on,
The nipple of her tit,
Oh Jesus Christ Almighty!

They had to memorise safe houses, names and addresses of contacts in the field, plus their codenames: Nancy was 'Hélène' to London, and 'Andrée' to the French, and had several other names for emergencies. She also knew that she was still 'The White Mouse' to the Gestapo. Major Farmer was to be called 'Hubert'.

The SOE 'dropped' their agents during the seven days either side of a full moon. The pilot needed the light of the moon to help pick out the bonfires lit by the Resistance fighters, which signalled where the parachutes, or 'umbrellas' as they were called, should land.

Some of the SOE agents would be sent into French towns; others, like Nancy, went to work with the Maquis, an unruly band of Resistance fighters, many of whom had run to the forests to avoid labour service under the Vichy Government. The Maquis were based in the Auvergne mountains in the middle of France – an area of hill-top villages, forests and harsh volcanic peaks. Nancy and Hubert's mission was to organise 'drops' of ammunition for the Maquis fighters, and train them in warfare, to help disrupt the German Occupation.

'Apparently they are very wild and sleep on piles of sticks in the woods,' said Major Farmer.

'I shall have to go into Vichy to wash my hair,' said Nancy.

'I don't think you'll be doing much of that,' said Major Farmer.

'Ah, come on,' said Nancy. 'A woman can't work in a forest full of Frenchmen without her hair done.'

Nancy thought Major Farmer would have found life easier if he could laugh at himself a bit more.

***

On the night they were due to go to France; Nancy and Hubert were dressed in civilian clothes, and taken to the airfield. The SOE even had a special fashion company to make their agent's clothes look French-made. Nancy checked her kit: torch, money belt, compass, knife to cut parachute, shovel to bury parachute, French ration 'tickets', French travel pass, French sanitary towels, and a Colt.32 pistol.

When bad weather stalled the flight for twenty four hours, even Major Farmer, who wasn't a party animal, agreed they should go and have a drink. A few hours later, Nancy and DenDen were doing parachute rolls along Piccadilly to Nancy's flat, singing: *'Glory, glory what a hell of a way to die'.*

'Don't you know there's a war on?' Londoners tutted as they passed by.

'Yes, we know,' shouted Nancy, as she rehearsed her parachute roll. 'Arm forward and curved, to break the fall, legs tightly together.'

'Why am I doing this again, Nance?' DenDen said, as they sobered up at her flat.

'Because you are committed,' she said. 'As am I.'

'Break a leg, sweetie,' said DenDen. 'It's an English expression for good luck.'

Nancy hoped they'd manage to link up with DenDen in France.

***

As Nancy was driven through London late the next evening, the headlights of the British army jeep shone out on the War Offices, where Army and Navy chiefs were working through the night planning the D-

Day landings – hundreds of ships were to surprise the Germans by landing on the beaches of Normandy. One of the first tasks for Nancy's team when they got to France was to blow up key targets which would disable German troops and tanks before D-Day in a month's time. She often wondered where Henri was; this time he wouldn't be there to support her resistance work.

At the airfield, Nancy and Major Farmer were met by Colonel Maurice Buckmaster, the head of the

French section of the SOE. He always gave his agents a parting gift and he gave Nancy a silver powder compact. Her ankles were then bandaged to break her landing, and Buckmaster issued his final instructions in a low, calm voice.

'A man called 'Tarvidat' should meet you. He's in

charge of 3,000 Maquis fighters,' he said.

Nancy was searched for any traces of Englishness: English cigarettes, bus tickets etc. Any suspicious item could attract the Germans' attention.

As the plane turned over its engines on the runway outside the hanger, Nancy was handed a suicide pill.

'Tuck it away in your lipstick,' Buckmaster said. 'Let's hope you don't need it.'

Major Farmer placed his in his pipe.

Buckmaster thought how stylish Nancy looked, even with her parachute strapped to her back. They met the pilot who was given another set of code names for them; Nancy was known as 'Witch' to the crew, not even they were allowed to know who they were really taking to France.

Nancy was one of 39 women in the SOE who were given missions in occupied France during the Second World War. It was quite a responsibility. As the plane took off into the moonlit spring sky in 1944, Colonel Buckmaster said a prayer to himself for their safety.

CHAPTER 6

'She is the most feminine woman I know, until the fighting starts. Then she is like five men.' Tarvidat

Nancy rubbed her ankles after an awkward parachute landing.

'The trees are a bugger,' said Major Farmer.

Sometimes he could be a bit smug, thought Nancy.

'*You* didn't land right in one,' she said.

As their pick-up car bumped along country tracks, they could just about make out the jagged mountain countryside in the moonlight. Nancy sat back in her seat, relieved to be back in France.

The Frenchman who picked them up was the Maquis leader, Tarvidat, a 30-year-old maths teacher and rugby player from the nearby town. He took them to a farmhouse for their first night.

Another local Maquis leader, Gaspard, watched Nancy pull out her frilly nightie.

'Do you intend to fight in that?' asked Gaspard.

'I'll fight them naked, if I have to,' Nancy said.

'I hope you're not going to be a nuisance,' he said.

'Because I am a woman?' asked Nancy

'Yes,' he said.

Nancy felt well-equipped after her SOE training, but she knew that she would have to prove herself as a woman if these wild Frenchmen were to respect her.

After the first night, Nancy and Major Farmer – 'Madame Andrée' and 'Hubert' to the French – were moved to a Maquis hideout in the Auvergne woods. The hideout consisted of camps covered in branches to hide them from the Germans.

By the time DenDen found them, Nancy was busy identifying the best 'drop zones' for the containers from London, which would bring ammunition for Tarvidat's men.

'What kept you?' said Nancy, as a rather dishevelled-looking DenDen was bought to their camp. 'Maybe I shouldn't ask?'

DenDen put down his heavy suitcase. It carried an all-in-one 'transceiver', which could send and receive radio messages.

'No, don't; are they all this good-looking?' said DenDen as he spotted Tarvidat.

Now that DenDen was with them they could send messages to the SOE in London to ask for guns and explosives to delay the Germans reaching the coast, and Colonel Buckmaster could tell them what he wanted them to do. While Hubert trained the Maquis in military tactics, Nancy took charge of organising the 'drops' which became more frequent as D-Day drew closer. Between 10pm and 4am, around the time of the full moon, Nancy and her men would sit in the dark, waiting. They would suck on loaf sugar soaked in plum brandy to keep warm, and lie in silence on the cold, wet grass. When they heard the drone of the warplanes overhead, they would leap up and light bonfires to signal where the plane should let go of its containers full of grenades, sten guns, and thousands of rounds of ammunition.

Once a month Nancy would have a special container sent from the SOE marked: 'PERSONAL FOR HELENE'. In it, would be her favourite Elizabeth Arden face cream, Brooke Bond tea, and chocolates — none of which you could get in France during the Occupation. Colonel Buckmaster didn't want his female agents to feel forgotten.

Nancy always made sure she was looking her best, even when she'd spent the night trying to sleep on a heap of bracken, which wasn't unusual.

'Want some?' Nancy jokingly offered Tarvidat her new lipstick.

'I didn't think Australians were supposed to be glamorous,' Tarvidat said.

'I am more French than Australian,' said Nancy

'You look more French than Australian,' said Tarvidat. 'Your husband should be proud of you.'

Nancy tried to comb her hair, which was full of twigs.

'He would laugh at me now,' she said.

It was when they had to wait for hours beside a railway line, or wait in the dark huddled around the radio transmitter that Nancy would wonder what Henri was doing. She preferred it when she was busy; then she didn't have time to think.

Nancy's organisation of 'drops' became so efficient, that even the surly Gaspard swallowed his pride, and asked Nancy if she would get his group ammunition from England.

'You seem to enjoy this work,' he said to her.

'We all enjoy work we are good at,' said Nancy.

Gaspard was a respected fighter among the Maquis

and Nancy knew she'd find a way to prove herself to him somehow.

***

The Allies landed on June 5th/6th 1944 – D-Day. The Maquis removed the axle grease from German rail transporters and replaced it with abrasive grease so they couldn't move. Nancy was ordered to collect an SOE agent who'd been sent to train the Maquis to use a bazooka. She was cross to miss blowing up the D-Day targets but, with this new weapon, she knew they could really finish off the Germans.

Following the D-Day landings, the Allied troops fought their way from the Normandy beaches into France. In the Auvergne, the Germans remained determined, and Nancy's group often found themselves in the line of German gunfire. Nancy would always hold out as long as she could, but in one attack they were so outnumbered by Germans, she had to jump into an escaping car, and carry on firing at the soldiers. A German fighter plane strafed Nancy's car with bullets from the air, and she threw herself from the moving vehicle to take cover in the hedgerows. Fearing that he might be taken prisoner, DenDen destroyed his radio code, and buried his transmitter.

Gaspard had observed how brave Nancy had been during the ambush.

'Alors, Andrée,' Gaspard said.

He took Nancy's arm and walked with her to safety.

'I think I understand you now,' he said.

'I'm glad,' said Nancy.

But without a radio, they were useless; without codes, London wouldn't trust their messages.

'I'm sorry,' said DenDen.

'I would have done the same,' said Nancy as she gave him her precious bottle of eau de Cologne to put on his bad leg wound.

Nancy volunteered to cycle to Chateauroux, where DenDen thought there might be an SOE operator who could call London for another radio set. It was a

400-kilometre round trip – about the same as cycling from London to Dublin.

She borrowed a long, white, cotton dress from a local farmer's wife – her femininity was to be her only weapon on this trip – and set off with no identity card. The Germans had clamped down on ID papers, and Nancy's were now invalid. She also didn't have a licence for the old farm bicycle.

'Did the eau de Cologne help?' Nancy asked DenDen as he attached a pretty string handbag to her handlebars.

'It definitely did,' said DenDen. 'I drank the whole bottle.'

Nancy wasn't in the mood for laughing.

'I wish the bloody brakes worked properly,' she said.

'It is imperative that when you're exhausted, and windswept, you do not *look* as if you are,' said Hubert. 'Good luck.'

Back in London they wondered why Hélène had gone so quiet. Colonel Buckmaster paced back and forth in the SOE headquarters.

'Any news?' he asked one of his officers.

'Nothing,' he said. 'You're fond of Hélène, aren't you Sir?'

'She's different,' Colonel Buckmaster said.

'She's probably drinking a German under the table somewhere,' said his colleague.

'Quite possibly,' said Buckmaster.

***

Round and round Nancy's tired legs went, up and down, over bumps on the road; her bottom hurt, and her legs ached, but Nancy cycled and cycled. She knew that if she got off that bike, it would take all her courage to get back on again. At each German checkpoint, she pretended to be a French housewife just off to the next village. She would look over to the Nazi officers, flutter her eyelashes and say:

'Do you want to search moi?'

They would laugh flirtatiously: 'No Mademoiselle, you carry on.'

So far, so good.

At Saint Armand, she heard that the Germans had just shot several hostages; this spurred her on to the next town, Bourges, where she bought some black market brandy to boost her flagging energy.

'Why is this country so hilly?' Nancy muttered, as the bicycle strained up another steep slope.

At last, after cycling for a day and a half through

enemy territory, Nancy reached Chateauroux. For the first time in her work for the Resistance, she felt scared, and very alone. German vehicles were gathered in the town square and any suspicious gesture made in occupied territory could mean death; Nancy was so tired she could barely walk.

DenDen's radio contact was a grumpy, bearded man, who refused to help her because she didn't have a password. Nancy took a big breath, pushed her bike calmly across the town square, past the soldiers who lent against their tanks. As she cycled away she could hear the screams of a woman being arrested by the Gestapo.

***

Back at Saint-Santin, the men sat round the fire.

'Will you sit down Denis,' said Hubert.

DenDen blamed himself for letting Nancy go off on such a dangerous mission. 'I know she's been caught,' he said.

'Nancy'll wow them,' said Hubert

'Then what?' said DenDen

***

Nancy cycled as fast as she could out of Chateauroux, by-passing the road blocks by going along a country track towards the woods outside the town where she knew there might be a Free French group. She could hardly speak from exhaustion when she came across a group of men in civilian clothes. The men were unsure of her to begin with, but they had a transmitter, and she persuaded them to send a message to Colonel Buckmaster asking him to send another radio for 'Hélène' as fast as possible. They could hear the German tanks leaving Chateauroux as the radio operator sent the message. Done. 'Mission accomplished,' she thought, 'thank goodness.' She climbed back onto the old bike.

'You came all the way from Saint Santin on that?' one of them asked.

'Yes,' Nancy said. 'And now I'm going back there.'

***

In central London, Colonel Buckmaster stared out of his office window at children in mucky vests scampering across rubble from a recent bombing raid. He was uncomfortably hot in his tweed suit. There was a knock at the door.

'Yes,' said Buckmaster, without turning round.

"Hélène' has made contact, sir. Needs a new radio.'

Buckmaster tapped his pipe on the windowsill, and returned to his desk.

'What are you waiting for?' said Buck. 'Send her perfume with it.'

The day was looking up.

***

Nancy's legs felt like lead. As before, she cycled non-stop; on and on, with terrible cramps in her legs, through the dark, seeing spooky shadowy figures which made her pedal faster and faster. When at last she saw the track towards the Maquis hideout she cried out with relief.

'You must rest,' said Tarvidat.

'Well done, darling.' DenDen couldn't stop hugging her.

Nancy couldn't talk, eat, drink, or sleep, she just cried with exhaustion.

'I shall never ride a bicycle ever again,' she said.

She had ridden just over 400 kilometres in 72 hours. The men heard that a plane was on its way, and Nancy slept soundly under the trees while they collected the drop – a brand new radio, complete with an operator called 'Roger', and a parcel marked: 'PERSONAL FOR HELENE'.

As she lay, resting, she wished that she could get a message to Henri; maybe he'd escaped to England by now.

***

The different groups of SOE agents would sometimes hear news of each other via their network. Nancy heard that her friend Violette Szabo had been captured shortly after she was dropped into France. She'd been taken to Ravensbruck concentration camp where the Germans would treat her as a spy; possibly remove her toe nails, starve her, or burn her with a red hot poker to make her talk. She'd also heard that O'Leary had nearly died in a concentration camp after being beaten. This made Nancy all the more focused on her work against the Nazis.

One day, she discovered that her Maquis men were holding three suspect women hostage and she intervened. Two of the girls were French, but the German woman, she realised, was a spy, and that meant one thing.

'Shoot her,' said Nancy to the Maquis.

The Frenchman prepared to shoot the woman as Nancy sat down to her breakfast. The woman tore off her dress and threw it on the ground in disgust. She spat at Nancy. The Maquis hesitated.

'What are you waiting for?' said Nancy

'They can't shoot a woman in cold blood,' said Tarvidat.

Nancy took a sip of tea. 'If you don't, I will,' she said.

'Aim,' shouted the Maquis.

The woman made the German salute: *'Sieg Heil!,'*

'Fire.'

Nancy knew that it would only take one spy to ruin the work they were doing.

'War is war – she had to be eliminated,' Nancy said to Tarvidat.

'Henri would be shocked, though.'

Nancy thought about Henri often, but she didn't talk about him.

'Your husband?' said Tarvidat.

'Yes,' said Nancy. 'I wonder if he'd believe some of the things I've done here.'

'You're doing it for France, and I am proud of that,' said Tarvidat.

'Yes, he would think the same,' said Nancy.

***

The French Resistance continued to sabotage the Germans as the Allies advanced across France. Tarvidat was Nancy's favourite Frenchman, apart from Henri of course. She loved fighting alongside him. On one occasion, they attacked a German ammunitions store. The idea was to take out the sentry while his back was turned.

'Go,' Tarvidat whispered to the Maquis. While he took one sentry, Nancy ran swiftly towards the other but he turned too soon; she felt a shooting pain in her arm as he lifted his shiny bayonet. In a flash, Nancy raised her other hand and brought it down in a karate chop on the man's neck. He slumped to the ground at her feet. Dead.

As Nancy lay beside his body, nursing the bayonet wound, she looked round for Tarvidat. 'It was him or me,' she said.

'We're lucky it was him,' said Tarvidat.

'The only good German is a dead one,' said Nancy.

She was surprised at herself when she said this out loud. But then she thought about what the Nazis had done to so many of her Jewish friends in Marseilles, and so many other innocent people.

With news that the Germans were beginning to retreat, Nancy decided that it was time for her to have a proper bed at night; she'd had enough of sleeping in rough camps. Resourceful as ever, she persuaded Tarvidat that it was safe enough now to find more comfortable headquarters.

'You're getting soft,' said Tarvidat.

'A woman needs to look after herself,' said Nancy.

'Leave it to me,' he said.

In the end, Nancy made a bed for herself in the back of the local double-decker bus with silk sheets made out of her parachute. This was heaven; the right way to fight a war. She pulled her regular sleeping partner towards her – a Sten gun, just in case there was a night raid from the Nazis – and turned over to go to sleep.

***

In August 1944, with the smell of freedom in the air, the German troops were becoming more disorganised. Many battalions tried to escape from France and retreat to Germany. Nancy, and her gang of Maquis, surrounded key battalions by blowing up bridges at strategic points along their route. They then joined Gaspard's army to help liberate Vichy. Pétain had been taken back to Germany as a virtual prisoner by the Germans, who were evacuating the town. Nancy and DenDen helped to restore order after the Gestapo left, shooting at civilians and looting shops as they fled.

Nancy moved her Maquis into an abandoned chateau, a large castle-type house, with a neglected garden – large enough for a 'drop'. On August 25th, Nancy's birthday, she and DenDen tuned in to the BBC News to hear that Paris had been liberated by the Allies. The Americans and the Free French had landed in the south of France, and the Germans were officially on the run.

'Hurrah!' shouted Nancy. She and DenDen waltzed around the large deserted dining-room in the chateau. 'What a birthday present!'

Nancy dressed up in her most elegant outfit – a silk dress made from her parachute – and was toasted by a table of drunken Maquis. She hadn't felt so happy since her wedding day. As she drifted off in a drunken snooze under the stars, she realised that for the past six months she'd only had about four hours sleep a night – she'd been so busy she hadn't noticed.

They returned to Vichy for another celebration. As Nancy danced around the square, she saw people she recognised from Marseilles.

'I can't believe all the hell has been worth it,' she said as they sat, drinking champagne.

'What are you going to do now it's over, Nancy?' said one of the women, a shopkeeper from Marseilles.

'I am going to find Henri,' Nancy said.

The woman was startled.

'Nancy, Henri was arrested by the Gestapo, last autumn.'

She paused, and looked away. Nancy felt as if someone had punched her in the stomach.

'I'm so sorry,' said the woman.

'He's dead, isn't he?' asked Nancy.

'I know people tried to find you.'

'I've been out of contact,' said Nancy.

Nancy couldn't tell them what she'd been doing; the

SOE's existence was top secret. DenDen saw she was upset, and led her away from the jubilant crowds.

'They killed him, because they couldn't find *me*,' Nancy said.

DenDen and Hubert helped her to navigate a route back to Marseilles. Many main roads and bridges had been blown up during the fighting. Marseilles itself had suffered the wear and tear of occupation, and many of its buildings were damaged. The Nazis had looted their flat and taken any valuables, except her most precious thing next to Henri – Picon. He'd been rescued by some friends, and looked after by them ever since.

Nancy discovered that Henri had been caught by the Gestapo in October 1943, shortly after she'd left him. He was tortured to death because he refused to tell them where 'The White Mouse' had gone. 'By the time they had finished with him, his kidneys were hanging out of his body,' reported the *Daily Telegraph* newspaper.

There was little point in sitting in the ransacked apartment – tidying up her affairs made her feel depressed. Nancy couldn't be in Marseilles and not think about Henri and what might have been. She took Picon for a walk around the old port – he never grew tired of chasing rubbish whipped up by the Mistral and she knew then that she couldn't stay any longer. She bundled Picon into the car, packed her remaining things, and they bumped their way back across France to join the others.

***

By the autumn of 1944 the liberation of France was almost complete. Only small pockets of German soldiers remained.

'Adieu,' Nancy said to Tarvidat and gave him a big hug.

'Au revoir Andrée,' he said. '*Au revoir,* please.'

It was difficult to say goodbye after such intense adventures.

DenDen, Hubert, and Nancy, plus an over-excited Picon, drove away from the Auvergne to Paris, where they found other SOE survivors. Nancy put on a brave face to attend yet another celebration party, but she kept thinking of Henri, and the loss of old friends, like Violette, who had been murdered at Ravensbruck concentration camp. Between May 1941 and 1944 the SOE had sent 39 women into France. Fifteen had been captured by the Nazis and imprisoned; only three of these had survived the death camps.

Luckily, O'Leary was alive, but frail, and was in Paris recovering.

'Would "The White Mouse" care to dance?' said DenDen.

'I can't believe I'll never dance with Henri again,' Nancy said, as they waltzed together.

'I know,' said DenDen.

Nancy was 33 when the war ended. She felt desolate.

'There is only one thing to do,' she said.

'Have a drink?' said DenDen

'Keep going,' said Nancy. 'Just damn well keep going.'

CHAPTER 7

'I want my ashes to be scattered over the mountains where I fought
with the Resistance. That will be good enough for me.'
Nancy Wake

During the war the work of the SOE was never mentioned in the newspapers, or on the radio. The adventures of its men and women agents remained secret. Later, some of them had their stories told in films – Violette's story was told in the film, *Carve Her Name with Pride* – or in books, but many of them went on to live ordinary, quiet lives. As Britain and France set about re-building their countries after the war, Nancy found work at the British Embassy in Paris, along with DenDen. But pushing passport papers from one desk to another was dull, and it felt pointless after her work for the Resistance. When Picon died in 1947, aged thirteen, Nancy felt it was the end of an era.

'I'll go anywhere, do anything, the North Pole – just give me an exciting job,' she said.

'Maybe you could train people in how to escape?' DenDen said.

He himself was hoping to find work as a steward on a cruise ship.

'I was just doing whatever I could, to help get rid of the Germans; now it's all just fizzled out,' Nancy said. 'But that escape idea isn't bad.'

'Let's drink to one of the most decorated Allied servicewomen,' said DenDen.

'Try saying that again by the time we've left this bar,' teased Nancy.

***

The British awarded Nancy the *George Medal*, and the French three *Croix de Guerre* – two with palm and one with star, and the *Medaille de la Resistance*. Later, they awarded her the *Chevalier de Legion d'Honneur*. The Americans awarded her their *Medal of Freedom* with Bronze Palm, and, more recently, the Australians made her a *Companion of the Order of Australia*.

In the 1950s she did teach escape exercises to pilots, in remote areas of England and Wales, for the Air Ministry. She threw herself into this new work, and only left because she met, and then married, Flight Lieutenant John Forward, a big drinking ex-bomber pilot with a great sense of humour.

When she was 63, Nancy went back to France to visit her friends from the Maquis. 'Tarvidat', who'd become a successful businessman in Paris, organised a lunch in her honour in the Auvergne – now an area popular for walking holidays. This time Nancy arrived by car, not by parachute and, as she approached the restaurant, passed groups of hikers enjoying the breath-taking mountain scenery.

'*Bienvenue à l'Auvergne! Ma chère amie,*' said Tarvidat.

'Tarvi!' shouted Nancy.

She was so glad to see her old friend again. He'd arranged for many of Nancy's friends from the Maquis to join them. He ordered the best wine, and they ate wild boar and local cheeses made from the milk of Salers cows, which live in the local mountain pastures.

'Shame we didn't eat like this 35 years ago,' said Nancy.

They sat on the terrace of the small hillside

restaurant for the rest of the afternoon, re-telling stories from all those years ago. As the sun began to set, Nancy swore she saw a red kite swoop along the steep side of the valley above them.

'I'm going to sell my medals,' she said.

'But they're important; they make us feel recognised,' said Tarvidat.

'I fought for freedom, not medals,' Nancy said.

The Maquis were keen to know what Nancy had been doing since the war.

'I've drifted,' she said. 'Embassy work, dabbled in Australian politics, but I've never really found that sense of purpose again.'

Tarvidat nodded in agreement.

'Can't see you as a politician, Nancy,' one of the Maquis said. 'You say what you really think.'

'You're right,' said Nancy. 'I tried golf after that.'

'That's the most boring sport on earth,' Tarvidat laughed.

'I still have a gin and tonic every morning with my cornflakes,' Nancy said.

'Since when have you eaten cornflakes?' laughed Tarvidat.

Shortly after the war Tarvidat had christened his baby daughter 'Nancy', and asked Nancy Wake to be her godmother.

'I hope she'll be as lucky as me,' said Nancy.

'I hope she'll be as brave as you,' said Tarvidat.

He raised his glass.

'A toast: To absent friends,' he said.

'To absent friends,' they chorused.

Nancy thought fondly about her dear Henri, and Marseilles, and her work with these men. She tried to understand how it was that she felt so alive when she was here, working with the Resistance.

The red ball of sun sank suddenly behind the hills. When I die, Nancy thought, I want my ashes scattered over these mountains.

***

November 2005.

Nancy Wake was widowed for the second time seven years ago. She did sell her medals, to pay for a stay in a top London hotel. Now, aged ninety three, she lives at the Star and Garter retirement home for servicemen and women in Surrey.

GLOSSARY

Allied servicemen – were on the side of the Allies in the war – these were Britain, France and the Soviets.

Aryan – in Nazi politics this means 'of Northern European origin' (typically blond and blue-eyed) and especially not Jewish.

Bazooka – a weapon, shaped like a tube, used against tanks.

Bayonet – a stabbing instrument of steel attached to the end of a firearm.

The Black Market – the secret trading of rationed food and other scarce products during the war.

Blitz – an overwhelming bombing attack from the air – specifically on Britain from September 1940 to May 1941.

Bren gun – a medium-machine gun.

Circuits – SOE and Resistance teams who were in Occupied territories.

Concentration camp – a place where Hitler kept his prisoners of war, sometimes called Death Camps.

Collaborate – to assist or cooperate with the enemy, especially an occupying force.

Cover – a disguise, a false identity, job, etc used as a front.

Courier – someone who carries money and messages to and from Resistance groups.

Curfew – a rule which says that people have to stay off the streets and go indoors at a certain time.

Demarcation Line – the line which divided France into

Occupied France and Vichy France.

Dispatcher – the man who gives parachutists a shove, to help them leave the aeroplane.

French Resistance – secret groups who worked to resist German rule and Occupation.

Gestapo – the Nazi secret police in Germany.

Free French – the group who, after the Occupation, continued the fight against Germany from within France. They were led by Charles de Gaulle who'd escaped to England when the Germans arrived.

The Front Line – the battle positions closest to the enemy.

Grenade – a small bomb thrown by hand.

Guerrilla warfare – harassing the enemy with small bands of fighters.

Henri Philippe Pétain – World War I military leader. He made a truce with Germany in World War II, and headed the Vichy Government, aged 83. He was sentenced to life imprisonment after the war, for helping the Germans.

Hitler – German leader who wanted world domination. He rose to power in Germany in the 1920s and 30s.

Informer – a person who passes on information against someone else.

Maori – a tribe in New Zealand.

Maquis – a Resistance group who worked in the forests of the unoccupied zone.

The Milice – a para-military force made up of French collaborationists, commanded by the Gestapo, whose job was to combat the French Resistance.

The Mistral – a violent, cold, dry north-east wind which blows in southern France.

Nazi – the word used to describe any member of Hitler's National Socialist party.

Occupation – when foreign troops move in to the territory of a defeated enemy to keep order.

Puttees – a cloth strip wound round the leg from ankle to knee, worn as a legging.

Refugees – people who run to another country for safety.

Sabotage – secret malicious action against the enemy.

Safe House – a place where people can safely hide.

Special Operations Executive – known as SOE, a secret British organisation set up to co-ordinate all action by way of subversion and sabotage against the enemy overseas.

Vichy Police – police who worked for the Vichy Government. They were quick to clamp down on anyone damaging the German war effort.

TIMELINE

1912   Nancy Wake is born in New Zealand (she then moves to Australia as a toddler).

1932   Nancy leaves Australia to go to Europe.

1933   German election is won by Hitler's Nationalist Socialist party.

1934   Nancy moves to Paris to work as a journalist. She buys Picon.

1936   Nancy meets Henri Fiocca.

1939   Hitler invades Poland. Britain and France declare war on Nazi Germany. Nancy and Henri marry in Marseilles.

1939-1940 The period known as the 'Phoney War' – everyone ready to fight but not much action.

1940   **May** Germany invades Belgium, Holland, Luxembourg and France. Henri is called up to fight.
        June The Nazis take Paris. Nancy begins work as a courier for the French Resistance. Italy invades Greece and Egypt.

1941   **June** Hitler invades Russia. Nancy meets Captain Garrow and helps with his escape line. She is wanted by the Gestapo for her work with the Resistance.
        December The Japanese bomb the US Navy at Pearl Harbor. The Americans join the war.

1942   Germans occupy Vichy France.
        The Gestapo arrive in Vichy France where Nancy is working.

1943	**January** The Milice is formed to hunt down the Resistance. Nancy forced to leave Marseilles.
	May Nancy arrives back in England.
	October Henri is arrested by the Gestapo in Marseilles.
1944	Nancy joins the Special Operations Executive.
	April 29th/30th Nancy dropped into Occupied France.
	June D-Day: the Allies land in Normandy.
	August The Allies land in the south of France.
1945	**April** Hitler commits suicide.
	May The Germans surrender.
	August The Japanese surrender.
1947	Nancy is awarded the American Medal of Freedom with Bronze Palm.
1948	Nancy is awarded the George Medal by the British.
1957	Nancy marries Flt Lt John Forward.
1959	Nancy and John move to Australia.
1970	Nancy is awarded the Chevalier de la Legion d'Honneur in France.
1980	Nancy re-visits the Auvergne and has reunion with Maquis.
1988	Nancy is awarded the Croix d'Officier de la Legion d'Honneur.
1997	John Forward dies. Nancy moves back to London.
2004	Nancy is awarded the Order of Australia.

QUIZ

After you've finished the book, test yourself and see how well you remember what you've read.

1. Nancy's favourite book was about a resourceful young woman called:
   Ava
   Abigail
   Anne

2. At the age of 16, Nancy ran away from home and:
   Joined a circus as a professional dog trainer
   Worked as a nurse in a small country town
   Became Australia's best female under-18 surfer

3. Nancy named her beloved terrier Picon after:
   A popular French drink
   Her favourite type of nut
   The middle name of Anne of Green Gables

4. What did Nancy wear for her wedding to Henri in 1939?
   A brand new leopard-skin pillbox hat
   A paint-splattered boiler suit
   A black silk dress made in Paris

5. In 1940 Winston Churchill set up the SOE, which stands for:
   Special Operations Executive
   Spies Over Europe
   Spanish Onion Enterprise

6. Nancy's first contact with the French Resistance was when she:
   Organised a protest against the Nazis in the fish market
   Met a man while having a drink in a bar
   Found a secret message in her take-away pizza

7. Nancy's first fake identity was as:
   An interior designer
   An aerobics teacher
   A doctor's secretary

8. To the Nazi police Nancy was known as:
   The Black Cat
   The White Mouse
   The Pink Panther

9. How many attempts to escape to Spain did Nancy make?
   4
   16
   22

10. In wartime London, English women were urged to:
    Dress well and wear make-up
    Only send one text message a day
    Learn German in case England was invaded

11. Nancy's favourite of the SOE's gadgets was:
    An invisibility cloak
    A cigarette gun
    A dart-firing watch

12. In order to make sure they could pass off as French people,
the SOE trainees were taught to:
    Say 'ooh la la' every time they sneezed
    Comb their hair in the French way
    Drink champagne for breakfast

13. As a secret code to identify herself to the SOE headquarters,
Nancy chose:
    A rude Australian limerick
    Twinkle, Twinkle Little Star
    The seven times table

14. The Resistance fighters called parachutes:
    Umbrellas
    Mushrooms
    Flying yurts

15. Nancy hid her suicide pill in:
    Her pipe
    Her lipstick
    Her diamond ring

16. When they needed a new radio transmitter, Nancy travelled 400 kilometres on:
    A milkfloat
    A bicycle
    A donkey

17. What did Nancy urge the Resistance fighters to do to a captured female German spy?
    Shoot her without delay
    Make her do all the washing-up
    Keep her locked up in a cellar until the war was over and she could have a fair trial

18. How old was Nancy when the war ended?
    23
    33
    53

19. After the war ended Nancy got a job in:
    The British Embassy in Paris
    The ladies' underwear department of Marks and Spencer
    A small hotel on the Isle of Wight

20. What did Nancy do with the medals she was awarded?
    Sell them
    Give them to the Army Museum
    Frame them and hang them in her loo

Author Biography

Lucy Hannah is writer-in-residence at HMP Rochester. This is her first children's book and she is currently writing a novel for adults.

Acknowledgement

Thanks to Terry Charman at the Imperial War Museum.

Dear Reader,

No matter how old you are, good books always leave you wanting to know more. If you have any questions you would like to ask the author, Lucy Hannah, about *Nancy Wake* please write to us at: SHORT BOOKS 15 Highbury Terrace, London N5 1UP.

If you enjoyed this title, then you would probably enjoy others in the series. Why not click on our website for more information and see what the teachers are being told? www.shortbooks.co.uk

All the books in the WHO WAS… series are available from TBS, Distribution Centre, Colchester Road, Frating Green, Colchester, Essex CO7 7DW
(Tel: 01206 255800), at £4.99 + P&P.